M000194642

"Some people understand the Holy Spirit as a .... concept, and their lives lack spiritual power and transformation. Others know the Holy Spirit intimately, as the person of God who resides in them. Their lives are marked by divine anointing and spiritual fruit. Mark Fuller knows the Holy Spirit intimately. I know of no one more passionate to see the church experience the powerful, personal presence of the Holy Spirit. Mark's Spirit-filled, fruit-bearing life inspires me not only to listen, but also to experience what he writes about in this book. "

—David Busic
Senior Pastor
Bethany First Church of the Nazarene

"Mark Fuller is a gifted pastor and leader. He has provided fulfilling ministry to some of our strongest churches. This volume reflects the fruit of his experience. His writing is both instructive and inspirational. He writes with clarity and conviction as well as the passion of an authentic shepherd desperate for his flock to fully enjoy this journey we call life. This book is ideal for the growing Christian who seeks God's best and refuses to settle for anything less."

—Paul G. Cunningham
General Superintendent Emeritus
Church of the Nazarene

"Pastor Mark Fuller has done an excellent job of presenting timeless truth in a new and refreshing manner. His book is very practical and easily understood. It will be especially helpful to the scores of people now attending our churches who have not been raised in Wesleyan-oriented churches. The study guide makes an excellent resource for Bible studies, small groups, and Christian education classes. This would be a wonderful book to place in the hands of every new convert."

—Thomas H. Hermiz
General Superintendent
Churches of Christ in Christian Union

"Great book! I enjoyed reading it and found it to be valuable for my life and understanding of the power of the Holy Spirit and how He wants to live in and through my life.

In today's world, where chaos and confusion reign, it is wonderful to read Dr. Fuller's words about the one and only resource we all need to know, embrace, and allow to flow through our lives—the Holy Spirit. The Spirit is the one person who can provide the answers we seek as we navigate a sometimes challenging and uncertain landscape of life. Mark's words provide a straight-forward, biblical perspective to understand the very nature of the Holy Spirit and how God wants to impact our lives with His presence so that we might fully experience the joy of life led by the Spirit and, in turn, live a life He can use to draw others toward Him."

—Dan Martin
President
Mount Vernon Nazarene University

"At last! A concise, direct, accessible book that unfolds the grace, power, and presence of the Holy Spirit, written from the life and love of a premier pastor who has walked with people just like you and me into the journey of the Spirit-filled life. Pastor Fuller provides this Scripture-based understanding of the Holy Spirit in a way that leaves me loving and longing for a still greater experience of His presence in my life. Thank you, Pastor Fuller, for extending your interesting, practical, pastoral teaching to our lives through this important book."

—Stanley W. Reeder
Superintendent, Oregon Pacific District
Church of the Nazarene

"With the mind of a scholar and the heart of a pastor, Mark Fuller explores the Person and work of the Holy Spirit. Few biblical truths have been so neglected and so misconstrued. With passion and purpose, Mark leads us to a clearer understanding of God's work through His Spirit. This book will preach!"

—J. K. Warrick
General Superintendent
Church of the Nazarene

CONSUMED

An Introduction to the Holy Spirit
Mark Fuller

BEACON HILL PRESS
OF KANSAS CITY

Library of Congress Cataloging-in-Publication Data

Fuller, Mark.
  Consumed : understanding the Holy Spirit / Mark Fuller.
    p. cm.
  ISBN 978-0-8341-2739-5 (pbk.)
  1. Holy Spirit. I. Title.
  BT121.3.F85 2011
  231'.3—dc23

                                             2011024606

10 9 8 7 6 5 4 3 2 1

Contents

Acknowledgments

I AM BLESSED to have been raised in a church that emphasizes the Person and work of the Holy Spirit and is sensitive to His leading. I am grateful that the Holy Spirit has revealed himself to me personally and that I experience His sanctifying work in my life every day. And I am humbled that God called me to live out this liberating good news to a culture hungry for the truth of the Spirit. I don't claim to be consumed by the Holy Spirit 24/7, but that is my heart passion and desire. I confess there are times I strive in the power of my own will and strength, but the Holy Spirit is faithful to remind that His presence and power is made perfect in my weakness.

I am grateful to Bonnie Perry and Nazarene Publishing House for their encouragement to put this sermon series into book form. God called me to preach, and I am much more comfortable communicating through that oral medium. But it is my hope and prayer that the message of *Consumed* will be an encouragement and resource not only to believers in their quest of knowing the Holy Spirit but also to my fellow pastors who call the Church to a Spirit-filled life.

I also want to acknowledge my father and mentor, Dr. Gene Fuller, who has not only exemplified life consumed by the Holy Spirit but has also championed the message of holiness as a leader in the Church of the Nazarene for six decades. I am grateful for the encouragement and support of my wife and life partner, Sue, whose life bears the fruit of the Holy Spirit far better than I.

Finally, I want to acknowledge the leadership of the Holy Spirit himself who prompted me to develop this series out of my own personal journey with Him. I wish I had the words to express to you the desire He has put in my heart for you to know Him deeply, intimately, and powerfully. Jesus said, "I have come that they may have life, and have it to the full" (John 10:10). May you experience Christ's abundant purpose for your life, and may you be consumed by His Spirit.

Mark Fuller

8

Introduction

THE HOLY SPIRIT is the least known and understood member of the Godhead. Consequently, the mere mention of His name creates a myriad of distorted images. Ask ten different individuals, and you'll likely get ten different answers about who and/or what the Holy Spirit is. For some people the name "Holy Spirit" conjures up images of something like Casper the friendly ghost. For others they bring to mind images like something from *The Exorcist*.

Because we fear what we do not understand, many of us have chosen to simply avoid the subject entirely. John T. Seamands, in his book *On Tiptoe with Joy*, tells of a preacher he once knew who commented that while he preached about Christ and God the Father, he never preached about the Holy Spirit. "I'm afraid to preach about the Holy Spirit—it may lead to fanaticism or emotionalism" was his reasoning. What a tragic perspective! The Holy Spirit is not someone to fear. If you're a Christian, then He is part of you.

Look at it this way. Suppose I receive a call from a pastor, and our conversation goes something like this:

"Mark, we want you to come to our church and preach a series of messages. But please don't bring your wife along."

"What? Why do you object to my wife coming along?" I reply.

"Well, we've heard that your wife has fits once in a while. And we're afraid she may have a fit in one of the services. We certainly can't afford to have that happen. I hope you understand."

"Sir, I don't know where you heard this news," I say in protest, "but my wife doesn't have 'fits.' That's someone else's wife you're talking about."

Similarly, when I hear someone attributing to the Holy Spirit that which is unseemly and ungracious, I feel like saying, "That's not the Holy Spirit you're talking about. That's some other spirit!"

At the other extreme are those who become so infatuated with the spiritual realm that they will embrace any book or teaching on the Holy Spirit without question. This kind of indiscriminate acceptance can lead to a lot of confusion and distortion of who the Holy Spirit is and how He works.

Both fear and naiveté are born out of a lack of knowledge. God tells us in His Word, "My people are destroyed from lack of knowledge" (Hosea 4:6). So for the next few chapters we're going to educate ourselves about the Holy Spirit. We're going to look at what the Bible teaches about who He is, what He does, and the difference He can make in your life. For many of you this will be an introduction to a dimension of God you have never before experienced.

ONE

Who Is the Holy Spirit?

THE INFORMATION AGE is a wonderful time to be alive. It's believed that today a person takes in more information in a few shorts years than a person living two hundred years ago did in his or her entire life. While having all this information at our fingertips is empowering, it comes with a price. Ask any doctor on the verge of retirement how different it is to practice medicine in an age when the average patient can attempt to know the intricacies of every ailment versus twenty-five years ago when such a thing was not even a dream. An overload of contradictory information can cause as much confusion as having no information at all.

In a few paragraphs we'll come back to the topic of spirituality in postmodern times, but for now it's enough to realize that before trying to gain a solid understanding of the Holy Spirit, we need to address a few myths about the Spirit that our current culture's spiritual infatuation has created.

Myth: The Holy Spirit is a thing.

In my conversation with people about the Holy Spirit's presence in their lives, I often hear them say things like "Have you got it?" or "Do you feel it?" as if the goal is to receive a certain experience or to somehow get zapped by God. Most of us would never refer to the Holy Spirit as a thing, but we often think of Him in impersonal ways. We see Him as some ethereal cloud that hovers over-

14

head or some mystical force that just sweeps over people, something like "the force" in *Star Wars*. The Holy Spirit is neither a force nor an impersonal phenomenon.

Reality: He is a person.

Scripture refers to the Holy Spirit as a person. In John 16 we find Jesus teaching His disciples about the Holy Spirit. In doing so, He continually refers to the Holy Spirit with the personal pronoun "He" or "Him." Notice just one verse, verse 13: "But when he, the Spirit of truth, comes, he will guide you into all truth. He will not speak on his own; he will speak only what he hears, and he will tell you what is yet to come." Seven times in this verse alone Jesus refers to the Holy Spirit as a person.

Anthropologists tell us that three attributes make up the personality: intellect, will, and emotion. God's Word tells us that the Holy Spirit possesses all three.

He has intellect.

The first part of Romans 8:27 affirms, "He who searches our hearts knows the mind of the Spirit." Jesus in speaking of the Holy Spirit said He would "teach [us] all things." Regardless of whether some of us have had teachers who seem to have had no intellect, teaching requires this very trait.

15

He has will.

The Book of Acts is not so much the acts of the apostles as it is the acts of the Holy Spirit *through* the apostles Consider Acts 16:6: "Paul and his companions traveled throughout the region of Phrygia and Galatia, *having been kept by the Holy Spirit* from preaching the word in the province of Asia" (emphasis added). On several other occasions we discover the Holy Spirit exercising His will. In Acts 13:4 Barnabas and Saul were "sent on their way by the Holy Spirit" or were "compelled by the Spirit" (Acts 20:22). All these things testify to the evidence that the Holy Spirit is a being who exercises His will.

He has emotion.

In Ephesians chapter four, the apostle Paul informs us why we should live holy and upright lives: "Do not grieve the Holy Spirit of God, with whom you were sealed for the day of redemption" (Ephesians 4:30). The Holy Spirit is grieved when we run roughshod over the mercies of God. Grief is a powerful emotion. You can't grieve an inanimate object. You can grieve only a person with feelings. So besides having an intellect and will, the Holy Spirit is a person with emotion. He is not a force, a mystical presence, or an entity. He is defined by who He is as well as what He does. As long as you primarily seek demonstrations of what He can *do*, you will perceive Him in an impersonal way. Yet He is a person to be loved, to share life with, and with whom to enjoy a personal relationship.

Myth: He is one among many spirits.

We live in the midst of a spiritual revolution. For generations the prevailing philosophy of enlightenment cast doubt and suspicion over the reality of the spiritual realm. From the era known as the Enlightenment through the period of Modernism, the ultimate test of reality passed through the laboratory. If it couldn't be proved in a test tube, it was neither real nor reliable. But not anymore. The last quarter century, a period we call Post-modernity, has seen a meteoric rise of interest in the spiritual world. Convinced that the meaning of life cannot be limited to the physical senses, the masses are turning to the unseen realm for answers. Consequently we have seen phenomenal increases in occult activity, increased interest in the supernatural and paranormal, and an infatuation with the New Age practices of channeling, astro-projection, and many other mystical practices.

In light of all this is a tendency to interpret the Holy Spirit in this same way, as if He is just one more spirit guide among a smorgasbord of options to help you discover the meaning of life. Yet the Bible makes it very clear that the Holy Spirit is not just one among many spirits at work today.

Reality: He is the third person of the Trinity.

The Holy Spirit is the divine Spirit, eternally coexistent with the Father and with the Son. *He is God.*

I readily confess to you that I cannot explain the Trinity to your satisfaction In fact, no one can. The fact that God is three-in-one transcends all human understanding. Regardless of that, we must understand that the Holy Spirit is God. He existed before Creation and was involved in the creative process. In Genesis 1:26 God refers to Christ and the Spirit when He says, "Let us make man in our image, in our likeness." Christian scholars are united in their understanding that the Holy Spirit *is* God. Whenever He is mentioned in Scripture, He is given the same honor and worship as are the Father and the Son. All the things we ascribe to God we also ascribe to the Holy Spirit. He is omnipotent (all-powerful). He is omniscient (all-knowing). He is omnipresent (all-present). He is not just one more spirit—He is God. He is infinite intellect, perfect will, and perfect emotion. And because of this, He works in perfect concert with the will of God the Father and the work of God the Son.

Another distortion along these same lines implies that the work of the Holy Spirit is somehow unique and different from the work of Jesus Christ. *Beware of any teaching on the Holy Spirit that departs from the work and ministry of Jesus Christ.* They are genuinely one in the same. Look at what Jesus says about the work of the Holy

Spirit in John 16:14: "He will bring glory to me by taking from what is mine and making it known to you." God the Father, God the Son, and God the Holy Spirit work in perfect harmony to reveal himself to us and His plan through us. The Holy Spirit is not just one more spiritual path to discover the meaning of life—He is the only One who can lead us to The Way, the Truth, and the Life. He is God himself revealed to us.

Myth: He is the power of God for special occasions.

The myth that the Holy Spirit is the power of God only for special occasions provides agreement to the fact that the Holy Spirit is God, but it erroneously asserts that the Spirit is His presence and power only at certain times and occasions. There are two prevailing opinions in the Church concerning the role and ministry of the Holy Spirit today.

1. Some maintain that the miraculous acts of the Holy Spirit demonstrated in the New Testament were for that era only. Their rationale dictates that those supernatural phenomena were necessary to birth the Church but ceased when the apostles died.

2. The other prevailing view is that the miraculous acts of the Holy Spirit are indicative of what He wants to do today. These acts play a role that is

just as important today as when the church was born two thousand years ago.

If Christ's great commission to "go into all the world and make disciples" is for us today as much as it was for His disciples then, it only stands to reason that the presence and power of the Holy Spirit are just as necessary today to fulfill Christ's great commission as they were back then. The Holy Spirit is not the power of God just for special occasions.

Reality: He is available 24/7.

If the Holy Spirit is not available at all times, how else could Jesus promise, "And surely I am with you always, to the very end of the age" (Matthew 28:20)? He said to His disciples, "Unless I go away, the Counselor will not come to you; but if I go, I will send him to you" (John 16:7). I don't think Jesus' disciples fully understood when He told them that it was *good* for Him to go away. They probably reasoned, "God has come to live with us in Christ. What could be better than that?" Yet just a few weeks later on the day of Pentecost, Jesus' promise came true: "In a few days you will be baptized with the Holy Spirit" (Acts 1:5). These same troubled and defeated disciples suddenly realized, "The God who came to live *with* us now lives *in* us as the Holy Spirit." Are you beginning to see God's wonderful plan to reveal himself to us and redeem His lost creation?

Adam and Eve enjoyed perfect intimacy and closeness with God in the Garden. But they sinned and disobeyed. Their sin destroyed that intimacy and brought separation from God. But God the Father immediately began building a bridge back to His fallen yet beloved creation. In the Old Testament *God spoke through His prophets.* And in the fullness of time, God came to Earth and revealed himself as the Son. In the New Testament Gospels *God spoke through His Son.* God is getting closer. He walked among humanity, lived with humanity, and suffered *for* and *with* humanity.

However, God moved a step closer two thousand years ago on the Day of Pentecost when He revealed himself as the blessed Holy Spirit. In both the New Testament and today, God speaks through His Spirit. The God who had walked *with* us now comes to live *in* us. You can't get more personal than that! That's the miracle of the Holy Spirit. He makes the promise of closeness and intimacy with God a reality—not just on Sunday but every day.

Is the light bulb turning on for you? Are you saying to yourself, *Wow—that's really what I need! I need the Holy Spirit to help me know that I am loved and close to God again. How do I get there? What do I need to do?* According to God's Word, simply ask. This is Jesus' promise for you today. "If you then, though you are evil, know how to give good gifts to your children, how much more will your Father in heaven give the Holy Spirit to those who ask him!" (Luke 11:13).

Throughout my years of dealing with people regarding their relationships with God, I've discovered many who testify, "I've trusted in Jesus as my Savior. I know He died for my sins, and I'm trying to live for Him." But the indwelling presence of the Holy Spirit is not a living reality to them. They understand the gospel in their heads and believe it in their hearts, but God still seems distant to them, and the Christian life seems unattainable to them. Those who are in this place need the witness of the Holy Spirit living within them. Jesus reminds us that receiving Him is as simple as asking God the Father for Him. When we open our hearts and invite the Holy Spirit to bear witness with our spirits that we are children of God, it is His promise to do so for all who sincerely ask with all their hearts. It is the Holy Spirit who makes real *in* us what Jesus Christ has done *for* us.

TWO

What Is the Work of
the Holy Spirit?

I GUESS as an author of a book on the Holy Spirit, it's probably a bad idea for me to recommend other works for you on this subject. But some works are so seminal to a subject that if you're really going to gain an understanding, you must know it. And that's the case here. The real challenge for someone like me writing a book like this is that the seminal work is pretty short and written by a major personality. In fact, chances are you probably have this book in your library. Of course, the book I'm talking about is the Bible.

"I thought you said it was a short book!" you may remark.

The part of the Bible dealing specifically with the Holy Spirit is remarkably short. It is the Gospel of John, chapters 14, 15, and 16. In this passage Jesus is teaching His disciples about who the Holy Spirit is. He goes through a list of characteristics that when we understand them give us deep insight into who the Spirit is and what He does. Let's look at that list as Jesus conveys them.

He counsels.

When the Spirit comes to take up residence in our lives, what does He do? Chapter 14 begins by telling us that the Spirit counsels. "I will ask the Father and he will give you another Counselor" (John 14:16). Other versions of Scripture translate that last word as "Comforter," or "Advocate." The original word is a combination of two

Greek words: *para*, which means "alongside," and the verb *coleo*, which means "to call." The Holy Spirit is called alongside.

Para clettos is a phrase originally used in a court of law. Let's say you're on the stand, the prosecution is pressing in on you, and you're feeling discouraged and overwhelmed by it all. So you call someone alongside you, an influential friend who has authority and clout in that court of law, who can speak in your defense. That's the picture Jesus creates of who the Holy Spirit is. He's the one called alongside you.

Why is He called alongside? He's called alongside to comfort us. When we're in trouble, when we're grieving, He's there to comfort us, to remind us that it's going to be okay. He's there to defend us when we're falsely accused and to strengthen us when we're weak. Right when we feel the weakest, He says, "Watch me work. That's where I do my best work. I'll strengthen you."

In this same verse in John, Christ uses a different word of which we need to take note. He doesn't just say "a counselor"—He says "*another* counselor." In the original language there were two words for "another." One word meant "another of a different kind." For example, if you bought a computer that didn't work when you got it home from the store, you might return it and get a different computer—a different model or brand. That second computer would be another of a different kind. But in this verse in John, that's not the variation Jesus uses. Instead, He's talking about *another of the same kind.*

When my daughters started college, they roomed together. As part of their high school graduation gift, I purchased a laptop computer for them. They were grateful but insisted that they *each* needed one.

I asked, "You can't share a computer? Your mother and I get along real well sharing a computer."

"No," they insisted. "We each have to have our own laptop."

So being the generous Dad that I am, I bought another laptop just like the first. I bought another laptop of the *same kind.*

This is the point Jesus is making. "I'm going to call alongside you another Counselor. He's just like the same Spirit you see in me," Jesus says. "Same person. Same presence in your life that's in mine." That had to be comforting to those disciples, because Jesus was talking about leaving them. He was saying, "Don't be afraid, guys, because once I go, the other counselor of the same kind—as you've seen in me—is going to come and live in you." He was talking about the Holy Spirit. And if you believe in Christ Jesus today, this same Spirit who lived in Jesus lives in you.

Think about this a second. Recall some of Jesus' incredible actions, His miracles of healing and resurrection. And now because we have this same Spirit within us, Jesus says we, "will do even greater things than these" (John 14:12). How can that happen? It's because the same Spirit in Christ lives in every child of God.

Jesus had just two hands. How many hands are represented by all of God's children? Greater things. Jesus had just two feet. How many feet are represented by all God's children? Greater things. Jesus had just one voice. We, having received the same Spirit, have millions of voices. The same Spirit who lived in Jesus lives in us as children of God, and through us He will accomplish greater things than when He walked the earth!

He abides.

In the last half of John 14:16 Jesus says the Holy Spirit will be with us forever. That's the Spirit of truth He's talking about. He's going to be with us *forever*—not just when we're at church. He's going to be with us on Monday morning and every morning, 24/7. The Holy Spirit doesn't just come to visit—He comes to stay. In the good times the Holy Spirit, child of God, is there with you. In the bad times the Holy Spirit is there too. When you feel Him, He abides. When you don't feel Him, He abides. When you're in a crowd, He abides. When you're alone and under pressure and nobody's around, He abides. He's still there. He hasn't left us. When we're walking through the valley of the shadow of death, He abides.

See—the question is not whether or not He abides. The question is whether or not you are acknowledging

His presence. Are you so preoccupied with your circumstances, what people are saying about you, what they're doing to you, that you can't even recognize His presence and what He's trying to say? Some of us waltz into church on Sunday morning and haven't even given Him the time of day all week long. Then we wonder why we don't feel His presence. We go days and weeks without acknowledging the abiding presence of the Holy Spirit, and we seldom learn to listen to Him. As we start looking for Him every day, we'll develop a sensitivity to the Spirit. We'll learn to recognize His voice over all the other voices.

He teaches.

Jesus also reminds us that the Holy Spirit teaches us. In John 14:26 Jesus says, "The Counselor, the Holy Spirit, whom the Father will send in my name, will *teach* you all things" (emphasis added).

I can be pretty slow to catch on sometimes, but according to Jesus, the Holy Spirit is going to teach me all things and will remind me of everything Jesus has said to me. I have good news for you today: you don't need to go to seminary to learn the deep truths of God. All you need is a teachable spirit and an insatiable hunger for the truth, and the Holy Spirit will teach you everything you need to know.

Spiritual truth must be spiritually discerned. How do you know that? Well, in 1 Corinthians 2:14 Paul writes, "The man without the Spirit does not accept the things that come from the Spirit of God." Now think about that. There are thousands of people today driving by churches on their way to the golf course or the lake or shopping, and they're seeing these parking lots filled and are thinking, *What in the world is that about?* They don't get it. You know why they don't get it? Because spiritual truths can be only spiritually discerned. The person without the Spirit does not accept these things, because they come from the Spirit of God. Those without the Spirit cannot understand things that are spiritually discerned.

Perhaps you can identify with this: before you came to Christ, you read the Bible, but it just didn't make any sense. Yet once you made that commitment to Christ, His Spirit came. Then you opened up the Bible—and the meanings of those stories just jumped off the page at you. Have you ever been there? That's the Holy Spirit who's taking the written word of God and is applying it to your life. He's speaking to you. So when you get out your Bible, you read something, and the Holy Spirit says to your spirit, "Stop right there."

We sometimes think, *I've got to get through my chapter here, God. I've got to read a chapter a day.*

No, don't do that. Work with Him. He has something He wants to say to you in those times. Just park right there and say, *Holy Spirit, help me to learn this. Help me understand.* Look at the point of those verses. If they're talking about trust, use a concordance and go back and read all the verses you can find on trust. You see, we have to learn to cooperate with the Holy Spirit. He will teach us. The Holy Spirit instructs us in the truth and reminds us of the truth. So nurture a teachable spirit. Stay sensitive, stay humble to His teaching, and He'll teach you everything you need to know.

He testifies.

The Holy Spirit also testifies. John 15:26 says, "When the Counselor comes, whom I will send to you from the Father, the Spirit of truth who goes out from the Father, he will testify about me." In the last chapter I warned you to be wary of any teaching about the Holy Spirit that sets itself up as separate from the ministry of Jesus. Here in John 15:25 we see The Holy Spirit and Jesus working together. They're not separate—they're the same. So now we find that the Holy Spirit confirms in us what Jesus Christ has done for us. When we say "Amen," it's another way of saying, "That's right." It's the work of the Holy Spirit to say "Amen" to the work of Christ. That's what Christ is saying when He tells us, "He will testify about me."

Now in verse 27, look at what Jesus says: "And you also must testify." Not only is the Holy Spirit testifying about Jesus—He also wants us to testify about Jesus. I think Jesus is putting these things together here for us because we have a role too. We have a part to play. And I can promise you that every time you testify about Jesus, the Holy Spirit's right there saying, "Amen." You may feel that your words are falling on deaf ears, but the Spirit of God is speaking to that friend who is hearing it. The Holy Spirit works with you on this.

So He testifies. And we join in that testimony as well. Always be ready to give a reason for the hope that you have in Christ Jesus.

He convicts.

The Holy Spirit not only testifies—He also convicts. "When he comes," Jesus says, "he will convict the world of guilt in regard to sin and righteousness and judgment," (16:8). Now, how many people are just as excited about the *convicting* work of the Holy Spirit as they are the *comforting* work of the Holy Spirit? I'm not always excited about His convicting work in my life, but I need it. Before the Holy Spirit can be my Comforter, He must be my *Discomforter*. We don't like it when the Holy Spirit comes and wags His finger in our faces. Sometimes He will say to me, "Mark, I want to deal with this in your life."

I have been guilty more than I care to admit of saying in return, "Holy Spirit, you're right. We need to deal with that, but I really have been reading about this lately. Let's talk about this together."

You know what He does? He says, "Mark, come here and deal with this now."

I know, Lord, but we'll get to that. You know, in my thinking, it would be so much better to take care of this other thing first—then we'll take care of that.

31

"Mark, take care of it now."

He's very insistent until I grieve Him to the point that I don't even hear His voice any more. Then I'm in real trouble.

We experience things like this every day. You've been working in the yard with the shovel, not wearing your gloves. You tell yourself that you're doing just a small amount of work. All of a sudden you feel a little pain. You look down and see that you have rubbed a blister. And it hurts. But you keep at it every day, and soon that blister turns into a callous. Now you won't feel anything. It's similar to what happens to our spirits. We continually chafe, resisting the promptings of the Holy Spirit and His convicting work. We get dull. We can come to church week in and week out. We can see people praising God. We can attend a worship service. We can hear the ministry of God's Word. The Holy Spirit is working in people's lives all around us, and we're not sensing God's moving. He's moving, and we don't feel a thing—because we have become calloused to the convicting work of the Spirit.

Sometimes it can be hard to distinguish the difference between the convicting Holy Spirit and the accusing of Satan, which is the condemnation of the enemy. By contrast, the Holy Spirit's conviction is specific and constructive in order to straighten up specific areas of our lives. Satan's work is to throw a vague cloud of condemnation over you. You just feel terrible. You don't know why—you just are. But the Holy Spirit is very specific when He's talking. That's the key difference.

Another thing too—demonic forces will try to destroy you. When you're hurting and you don't know what the problem is, there's nothing more disconcerting and likely to send you into despair. That's the enemy's attempt. He wants to destroy you. He wants to throw this blanket of guilt and condemnation on you. He wants to accuse you. "Yeah, you'll never amount to this. You won't amount to that. You won't measure up to that standard." That's the accuser.

But the Holy Spirit says, "Look what I can do. Trust me. Work with me. Repent. Don't do that. Do this."

When you break your arm, there's significant pain. But once that bone is set and the cast is put on, in a few days there's another lesser pain associated with that. We realize this second pain is a good hurt, because we know the bone is mending. In the same way the Holy Spirit can help you discern the difference between a bad hurt and a good hurt. Both hurt. But one is of the Holy Spirit, the other of the accuser.

So many people are taught to avoid the word "sin." We talk about our shortcomings. We talk about our dysfunctional emotions. We talk about our Irish temper. But you know what? It's called *sin*. We need to learn to call it what it is. And the Holy Spirit convicts us when we sin. Sin occurs when we know what God wants us to do and we willfully and intentionally decide to do something else. Don't blame it on your ancestors. Don't blame it on your temperament. It's *sin*. And it's the Holy Spirit who says, "That's going to destroy you. Stop it."

I was talking with somebody recently who was making some decisions that were just tremendously destructive in his life. He said when he had begun to make those decisions, he had been feeling pretty good about them. When I laid it out there straight and told him about the consequences of disobeying what he knew God desired, he began feeling terrible. In all likelihood it wasn't me who made him feel terrible—it was the Holy Spirit. Again, He has to be our Discomforter before He can be our Comforter. God loves us too much to let us get away with our sin. It cost God the best He had to take care of our sin problem, and we need to work with the Holy Spirit on this.

The Holy Spirit also convicts us in regard to righteousness. Sometimes we can start to think that our own righteousness is pretty good, but the Holy Spirit reminds us just how lacking our righteousness is compared to His. Some years ago I remember a detergent commercial in which a person held up a towel washed with the competitor's brand of detergent. By itself it looked really clean and white, But when one washed with the advertiser's brand was held up next to it, the towel washed in the other brand of detergent suddenly looked dingy and yellow.

The Holy Spirit does the same thing for us. When we hold up our righteousness alone, we might look pretty clean. But when we compare it to *His* righteousness, we see how dirty and stained we really are. It is the Holy Spirit who convicts us of our need for His divine detergent to cleanse our hearts from sin.

Finally, the Holy Spirit convicts us regarding judgment, because the prince of this world stands condemned. I love this aspect of the Holy Spirit. He convinces me and convicts me when I forget that Satan has lost. I need the Holy Spirit to come alongside me and say, "Mark, don't despair. I don't care how bad it looks now. I don't care what's going on in the world around you. I don't care how much you've been falsely accused. I want you to know that I'm greater in you than he who is in the world."

It's the Holy Spirit who bears witness with my spirit when He says, "Affirm my presence. Remind yourself: Satan is defeated. The prince of this world stands condemned. Satan wants to defeat you. He wants to bury you. You have no rightful place with Satan and his minions. You are a child of God. You belong to Jesus. You are destined for the throne. You are more than a conqueror through Christ Jesus, who loves you." In the final analysis of things, everyone who trusts in Him shares in His victory.

So He abides, He teaches, He counsels, He testifies, He convicts. He also guides.

He guides.

Jesus tells us, "But when he, the Spirit of truth, comes, he will guide you into all truth" (John 16:13). In the same way that a guide leads and directs people along an unknown trail to the desired destination, so the Holy Spirit is our true divine guide to lead and direct us along the unknown paths of life. Have you discovered yet that the world today is confused about what is truth and what is error? Many people are so confused that they conclude that objective truth is impossible to know. These people feel that the best you can do is to decide what truth is for you individually. But trying to find our own way leaves us even more lost and confused. The wisest man who ever lived, other than Christ, astutely observed, "There is a way that seems right to a man, but in the end it leads to death" (Proverbs 14:12). From our limited perspective we make decisions about what is right with only limited information and limited knowledge. At first our decisions may seem right, but ultimately they will lead to destruction

Years ago I had the privilege of attending a world youth conference in Switzerland as a member of a singing group. During a week of orientation we took a hike along a mountainous ridge of the beautiful Swiss Alps. As young, energetic college students, several friends and I were becoming agitated at the slow pace of the group of "middle-agers" we were with. We asked the guide if we could pick up the pace and go on ahead. He resisted initially, but after our continued pleading, he reluctantly consented and gave us clear instruction to follow the red-and-white marked trail to our destination. So we bolted ahead, glad to be freed from the tether of slow hikers. About an hour later we came to a fork in the trail. Oddly, both trails were marked red and white. We were in a dilemma because we had outpaced our guide who could show us the right way. From our impatient perspective, waiting for him to arrive with the rest of the group was out of the question. So together we determined *a way that seemed right to us.* For the next hour or so it seemed right. But slowly the terrain began to change. The trail increasingly deteriorated and became treacherous. By the time we realized we had made the wrong choice, it was too late in the day to turn back and retrace our steps. There we were, stuck in the middle of the Swiss Alps, lost and without a guide. That memory has come back to me as a vivid illustration about the importance of staying in touch and on pace with the Holy Spirit as I journey along life's path.

"There is a way that seems right to a man, but in the end it leads to death." It may seem like a dramatic statement, but the natural human choice is almost always the wrong choice. Why? Because that choice is made from a fallen mind-set and a limited perspective. Jesus knew that His disciples would need a Guide to lead them into the truth. He knows that we need a Guide as well. And the sooner we learn to stay on pace with our Holy Spirit and follow His directives, the more enjoyable the journey will be.

He confirms.

"He will not speak on his own; he will speak only what he hears, and he will tell you what is yet to come" (John 16:13). Jesus isn't saying that the Holy Spirit gives us the ability to see the future; rather, He is referring to an understanding that the Holy Spirit was to give His disciples about the imminent future of His death and resurrection. "He will bring glory to me by taking from what is mine and making it known to you" (John 16:14). In other words, it is the role of the Holy Spirit to make real and personal the significance of what Jesus Christ did for you through His death and resurrection

We've already observed that the Holy Spirit testifies to the work of Jesus Christ. Here in this context, Jesus says that the Holy Spirit "confirms" that same work in our hearts. Are you beginning to see how the entire Godhead—Father, Son, and Spirit—are at work in this confirming process? Jesus tells us in verse 15, "All that belongs to the Father is mine. That is why I said the Spirit will take from what is mine and make it known to you" (John 16:15). Everything that belongs to the Father has been given to the Son, and the Holy Spirit makes it known to you and to me. The Father *initiates* our salvation. Jesus Christ *mediates* our salvation. The Holy Spirit *substanti-*

ates our salvation. It is the work of the Holy Spirit to confirm the love of God in Christ Jesus to you.

Have you ever read the Bible or listened to someone preach the Word or been in prayer—and it's as if a light comes on in your mind and heart? You suddenly say to yourself, *I get it—now I understand what it means!* The light comes on. That is the confirming work of the Holy Spirit. Remember: spiritual truth must be spiritually discerned. You can know the facts but still miss the truth unless the Holy Spirit confirms it in your spirit.

Recently I was getting acquainted with one of my church members and asked him how he came to the Lord. He told me that he had been raised in church, was taught the Bible, and even had parents who modeled Christianity for him as he was growing up. But the concept of an intimate, personal relationship with God never made sense to him. Christianity to him was nothing more than a religious activity, living a good moral life, and helping out people in need. It wasn't until a personal health crisis forced him to face his own mortality that he suddenly realized how little control he truly had over his life. In that teachable moment the Holy Spirit confirmed to him what Jesus Christ had done for him.

He told me, "Pastor, I had always believed that Jesus died for the sins of the world, but it never meant anything to me. In my brokenness I realized that Jesus died for me. It was my sin that nailed Him to the Cross. In that divine moment of revelation, I repented of my sin and invited Christ to take control of my life." The light came on for him. What was simply a religious activity became a vital personal relationship with God in Christ Jesus. That is a great example of the confirming work of the Holy Spirit in our lives.

Jesus has taught us several things about the Holy Spirit here in John 14-16. He counsels, He abides, He teaches, He testifies, He convicts, He guides, and He confirms the truth in our hearts. But the New Testament tells us there are at least three other areas in which the Holy Spirit is at work in the lives of believers.

He sanctifies.

"[Christians] who have been chosen according to the foreknowledge of God the Father, through the sanctifying work of the Spirit, for obedience to Jesus Christ and sprinkling by his blood" (1 Peter 1:2). It is the responsibility of the Holy Spirit to sanctify you. "Sanctify" actually means "To set apart for God's holy use." When you totally commit your life to Christ, the Holy Spirit begins a radical overhaul process in you to make you fit for God's use. We'll look more closely at how He does this in the next chapter. But let me emphasize here that you can no more sanctify yourself to God than you can save yourself from your sin. Just as Jesus died on the Cross to forgive you of the guilt of your sins, He also died on the Cross to break sin's power over you, that you might be sanctified (set apart) unto God as well.

Look at this verse: "Jesus also suffered outside the city gate to make the people holy through his own blood," (Hebrews 13:12). It is the work of the Holy Spirit to effect that sanctifying work in your life for God's glory. And when He sanctifies . . .

He also empowers.

Jesus also gives us another clue to who the Holy Spirit is. In Acts 1:8 He says, "You will receive power when the Holy Spirit comes on you." Notice He says you will receive power *when* the Holy Spirit comes on you. This enabling power accompanies the living, dynamic presence of the Holy Spirit in your life. And notice, too, that this power is for a specific purpose: "You will be my witnesses in Jerusalem, and in all Judea and Samaria, and to the ends of the earth" (Acts 1:8). The Holy Spirit's power is designed to give you boldness and a confidence that says to a lost world, "I have discovered the purpose of life—so can you. Let me share Him with you."

If you are seeking the power of God, you will never discover it. On the other hand, if you are seeking the Holy Spirit of God with all your heart, you will receive Him and His enabling power to be a bold witness to your world.

He intercedes.

The *word* "intercede" means to plead for someone else. In the New Testament it is almost always used in the context of prayer. There are many times when I don't know how to pray. My heart is set on God, but I feel very weak, confused, and powerless. It is in those times that I recall Romans 8:26-27: "In the same way, the Spirit helps us in our weakness. We do not know what we ought to pray for, but the Spirit himself intercedes for us with groans that words cannot express. And he who searches our hearts knows the mind of the Spirit, because the Spirit intercedes for the saints in accordance with God's will."

The point Paul is making here is that you cannot have real prayer apart from the Holy Spirit. He essentially says, "Left to ourselves, relying upon our own wisdom and resources, we know neither the 'how' nor the 'what' of real prayer." But God knows our human weakness and has given to us His Holy Spirit to help us. It is the Holy Spirit who brings both the impulse and the insight for prayer.

All effective prayer is in harmony with the will of God—and the best way to pray God's will is to pray His Word. Reading the Bible while you pray will ensure that you are staying on track in your prayers. And as you read, the Holy Spirit will give you insight as to how to pray. So keep praying. "Pray continually" (1 Thessalonians 5:17). Even when you don't feel like it and especially when you don't know how to pray, keep praying. For God's Word tells you that the Holy Spirit intercedes for you. He takes your sincere, honest, and heartfelt prayer and fashions it so that it comes out right in God's ears. The good news is that you don't have to have it all figured out. Just pray. Just worship. Just continue to pour your heart out to God. And the Holy Spirit will plead for you to the Father.

Through the years many things have happened in my life that did not make sense to me at the time, and I didn't know how to pray. But I simply poured out to God all my confusion, sorrow, pain, and even anger. As long as I kept my heart set on Him, an amazing thing happened: those happenings didn't drive me away from Him—they drew me closer to Him. That's the work of the Holy Spirit. He gives me grace to cope with the loss. He reminds me of the Father's love. He gives me strength to sustain me when my strength is gone. He increases my capacity to love and be patient. And He is here to help you pray today.

THREE

How Can I Be Filled with
the Holy Spirit?

IN JOHN 14-16 Jesus tells His disciples that it was a good thing for Him to return to heaven. You see, the disciples had walked with Jesus for three years. They had seen Him do incredible miracles. And when Jesus started talking about leaving them, that made them sad. But He explained, "It is for your good that I am going away. Unless I go away, the Counselor will not come to you; but if I go, I will send him to you" (John 16:7). In Acts 1:4-5 we also find Him telling the disciples, "Do not leave Jerusalem, but wait for the gift my Father promised, which you have heard me speak about. For John baptized with water, but in a few days you will be baptized with the Holy Spirit." Essentially Jesus was saying, "John took you under the water, signifying your faith in me, to wash from you the sins of your life. In the same I'm sending my Spirit to cleanse you from the actual sinful nature that you were born with."

Being filled with the Spirit is a divine imperative. Yet I often find among Christians those who say, "I love Jesus Christ. I live for Him. I go to church. I believe Jesus died on the Cross for my sins. But I don't know about this Holy Spirit thing." There's a notion among many Christians that being filled with the Holy Spirit is kind of optional equipment, as if we were buying a new car and choosing what to take and what to leave behind. Many people have this attitude that says, "I'm a standard Christian, whatever that is. You know I'm not ready for this deluxe package here"—or "That's not for me. It costs too much." But there's nothing biblical about that distinction.

Look at what God's Word says in Ephesians 5:18: "Do not get drunk on wine, which leads to debauchery. Instead, be filled with the Spirit." Now Paul uses the strongest language he could use here. It's a divine imperative, not an option. And it's not just for those who want to get serious about living for Christ. It's a divine imperative for everyone—*be filled with the Spirit.*

God has affirmed this throughout all time. In the Old Testament He called his people to holiness, to be set apart for His holy use. He said, "Be holy, because I am holy" (Leviticus 11:45). Centuries later, through His revealed Son, Jesus Christ, He reiterates this imperative: "Be perfect, therefore, as your heavenly Father is perfect" (Matthew 5:48). Again in the new Church era, the apostle Peter reminds us, "Just as he who called you is holy, so be holy in all you do" (1 Peter 1:15). In all you do—not just on Sunday morning when you're in a worship service. In *all* you do be holy.

Do those verses make you as uncomfortable as they do me? I read those and say to the Lord, *God, what are you trying to do to me? I was already feeling guilty before I went to prayer today. Now I really feel guilty, because I know I'm not holy. I know I'm not perfect. And yet you say in your Word, "Be holy, because I am holy." "Be perfect, therefore, as your heavenly Father is perfect." How in the world does that happen?*

Well, I can tell you how it *doesn't* happen. It doesn't happen through our own efforts. It will not happen because we try to be holy people. It is impossible to live a holy life without the fullness of God's Spirit living in us. We can no more make ourselves holy than we can forgive our own sins. Yet being holy is His imperative. It is His work.

I think this is the reason so many people get frustrated with the Christian life. They're trying so hard to live a Christian life, and it's not working. And that's the problem. They're trying—on their own. We need to try less and trust Him more. We need to take God at His Word. The reason God commands us to be filled with the Holy Spirit is because He knows there are no other resources whereby we can fulfill His command to be holy.

And this is the next truth: this is not only a divine imperative—it's a divine obligation. It is not some human opinion—it is God's obligation. 1 Thessalonians 5:23-24 says, "May God himself, the God of peace, sanctify you through and through. May your whole spirit, soul and body be kept blameless at the coming of our Lord Jesus Christ. The one who calls you is faithful and he will do it." That covers everything, doesn't it?—spirit, soul, and body. He wants to sanctify us from the top of our heads to the bottom of our feet. And here's the best part: "The one who calls you is faithful and he will do it." God is obligated to pull this off in our lives if we'll be open and trust Him and His promise.

He will accomplish this in different ways. He will accomplish this in as many different ways as there are different people. For some, He'll accomplish it in a moment in time. We'll come to Him, come to Christ as our Savior, and very quickly we'll come to trust Him in the fullness of His Spirit in our lives. Others will receive the baptism of the Holy Spirit after many years of being a Christian. Some testify to a vivid, spectacular event in their lives. Others testify to a quiet yet deep, peaceful assurance. The point is—don't get caught up in how it will happen for you. The Holy Spirit will deal with you in a very individual way. The important thing is that you don't miss the reality of being filled with the Holy Spirit.

How are we filled with the Spirit?

God deals with us individually, but there are a few distinctions in how we are filled with the Holy Spirit that you should be aware of.

First, we cannot be holy without being filled with the Holy Spirit. Remember in John 3 when Nicodemus came to Jesus at night and Jesus explained about the Kingdom: "I tell you the truth, no one can see the kingdom of God unless he is born again . . . born of the water and the Spirit" (John 3:3, 5). So there's an aspect of being *born* of the Holy Spirit. But in other places the Bible also says we can be *filled* with the Spirit. What's the difference between being born of the Spirit and being filled with the Spirit?

The Spirit of God comes to take up His dwelling in our lives the moment we accept Jesus Christ as our Savior. The Spirit bears witness with our spirits that we are children of God. So that's being born of the Spirit. But what does it mean to be *filled* with the Spirit?

First, let's talk about what it *doesn't* mean. It doesn't mean that we get a little bit of Him when we get saved (which is another way of saying "born of the Spirit"), and then we get the rest of Him when we get entirely sanctified, or filled with the Spirit. No, when we truly place our trust in Jesus Christ, we receive *all* of the Holy Spirit in that moment. But though we have all of Him, He doesn't yet have all of us. Being filled with the Spirit doesn't mean that I get more of Him—it means that *He gets all of me.*

Some people continually pray, *O God, I want more of you. Give me more of you.* You know what God's saying? "Hey, wait a minute. You *have* all of me—*I* want all of *you.* Once you give me all of you, then you'll experience the fullness of me." Being filled with the Spirit is the difference between Jesus Christ as your Savior and Jesus Christ as your Sovereign. It's one thing to trust Jesus to forgive you of your sins, but it's quite another thing to get out of the driver's seat and give the Holy Spirit control over your life. This is what the apostle Paul was talking about when he wrote, "I consider everything a loss compared to the surpassing greatness of knowing Christ Jesus my Lord" (Philippians 3:8). When this happens, Christ reorients our priorities. He turns our lives upside down. The things we thought were so important don't mean anything anymore. He changes our thinking.

Many people I meet profess Jesus Christ as their Savior, but few are willing to make Him truly their Sovereign. If we want to be filled with the Holy Spirit, that has to happen. Being filled with the Spirit is the difference between the Holy Spirit as our resident and having Him as our president. When we invite Christ into our lives, His Spirit comes to take up residence in us. But He's not yet president. What if He says to you this week, "You know this house that you've invited me to live in? I want to knock down a few walls here. I've got a major remodeling project to begin." How would you feel about that? "What about that closet you don't want to show me? You've invited me into all these rooms, but there's a closet down in the basement you've been hiding from me. I want to see what's in there." When we give Him everything, that's when He truly becomes president of our lives. It's one thing to acknowledge His presence. It's quite another thing to completely submit to His will in every area of your life. Yet this is exactly what the apostle Paul testified to. He said, "If your sinful nature controls your mind, there is death. But if the Holy Spirit controls your mind [if he controls your mind in every part of your being], there is life and peace" (Romans 8:6, NLT).

We've seen so far that being filled with the Holy Spirit is God's clear command. It's His initiative. It's His imperative. He also assumes the responsibility to do this work in our lives. And we see the difference between being born of the Spirit and being filled with the Spirit. So now all of this begs the question: how can we be filled with Spirit?

I'm so glad you asked.

Let me suggest an acrostic of the word "FILL" to help you remember. First of all, if we want to be filled with the Spirit of God, we have to **F**ace the root of the problem. We'll never be filled with the Holy Spirit until we acknowledge our basic sinfulness. This is the direction we receive in 1 John 1:9: "If we confess our sins, he is faithful and just and will forgive us our sins and purify us from all unrighteousness." So God promises to forgive and purify us. But before He can purify us, we have to acknowledge and confess our sin.

We're not sinners because we sin. We sin because we are sinners. There's a big difference. We need to acknowledge that the sins we commit flow from a deep problem within us. Our hearts are set against everything God is. When left to our natural tendencies, we will not do what God wants us to do, because we're fallen from grace. This is the sinful nature we're born with. When we act on that sinful nature, we incur guilt. God forgives us of our sins. But He also wants to cleanse us from all unrighteousness.

To receive forgiveness means we must repent and confess to God the sin in our hearts. All of us go our own directions in life, living the way we want to live, and God tells us to go another direction. Repentance means you stop in your tracks and turn around and head straight toward what God wants in your life. When we give ourselves to God, it's like surrendering; it's going from being a willful rebel to where we quit fighting God and raise the white flag. We decide we're not going to fight God any more. That's what Saul did on the road to Damascus. He was willfully rebelling against God when God knocked him off of his horse. When Paul had this discussion with God, he essentially said, "I surrender. I wave the white flag. I'm not going to fight you anymore."

After we repent, we need to confess our sin. Confession means to verbalize our repentance to God. It's telling God we can't control the sin problem in our lives. We admit to God that we realize that only He can make things right in our hearts. When we come to that place, God will forgive us of our sins and cleanse us from all unrighteousness. That's His promise. He will do that, but we have to face the root of the problem. This is what Paul meant when he said, "I have been crucified with Christ" (Galatians 2:20). Paul saw himself on a cross dying to his own will. Dying to ourselves is no easy proposition. But once you begin that process, continue on through it. Because on the other end of that crucifixion you're going to find the resurrection power of the Holy Spirit born anew in your life. He will fill you with all you need to live for Him.

Maybe you've done that. Maybe you're in a place where you think, "I've done that, but that old sinful nature raised its ugly head the next week." That's exactly what happens, so we need to die out every day. Paul encouraged us to die every day. Now if this was the testimony of arguably the greatest Christian who ever lived, what about us? We have to die every moment—not just daily. We have to get this thing down moment by moment by moment. We must continually crucify the self that wants to raise its ugly head in our lives, render it powerless, so that we can be raised to life in Christ and experience and live in the fullness of his Spirit. We must face the root of the problem.

If you've asked Christ to forgive you of your sin but you find that every day you're back where you started, then this is your next step. As important as forgiveness is to make us clean, once we're His children it becomes just a Band-Aid rather than a permanent solution. If you're reading this book, you probably don't need another Band-Aid to make you feel a little better. You don't need a talk on positive thinking. To experience the fullness of this life He has for us, we must die out to ourselves. And when we do that, God will hear our prayer.

Second, once we've faced the root of our problem, we must Invest our entire devotion to God. This is what Paul says in Romans 12:1: "I urge you, brothers, in view of God's mercy, to offer your bodies as living sacrifices, holy and pleasing to God—this is your spiritual act of worship." Is God number one in your life? Does He have complete control of your life? Can He do anything He wants to you?

A few years ago I had to come to grips with this again. I committed to Him long ago, but I have to keep committing. I have to do this every day. When God started tapping me on the shoulder, telling me to leave family and friends and a home of eighteen years in sunny, warm Arizona and go to Grove City, Ohio, I had to die out to myself. I had to work through it again. I had to say, "God, you can really do anything you want to do in my life."

Does He have that kind of control over you? Have you given Him that? Just sit down with your calendar today, and look through what you are spending your time doing. Does your calendar show that God is the most important person in your life? What about your relationships? You will never experience the fullness of God's Spirit until you invest your entire devotion to Him.

Third, to be filled with the Spirit we must Look to Christ's cross. In the last chapter we learned that Jesus died not only to wash away the stain of the guilt of our sins but also to break the power of sin over our lives, to sanctify us, to make us holy the way God has required us to be. Look at this: "Jesus also suffered outside the city gate to make the people holy through his own blood" (Hebrews 13:12). Everything you need from God was purchased by Jesus on the Cross for you—everything. Your salvation, your sanctification, your healing, your deliverance—everything is right there in the cross of Jesus Christ.

As a college student I used to try so hard to convince God to sanctify me. I wanted to be filled with His Spirit. I was trying everything I knew. I prayed for an hour or two hours a day and hoped it would lead to me being sanctified by the Holy Spirit. I would promise God that I would study His word harder than ever. I was looking for this tingling up and down my spine, some sign that I got it. I did everything—everything, that is, but trust Him.

As long as I was trying, I was in the way. It was my efforts to get sanctified that were actually preventing me from experiencing it. But when I quit trying and just trusted Christ, then He was able to do His work. My part is to trust God with my life. The Holy Spirit's part is to sanctify my life to God. To be filled with the Holy Spirit we must Live in humble obedience to Him. Remember: the Holy Spirit is a person. This is our life-long relationship with a person who is deeply loved and cherished. Being filled with the Holy Spirit requires a commitment to continually follow His leading.

Look what else Paul says: "Do not grieve the Holy Spirit of God, with whom you were sealed for the day of redemption" (Ephesians 4:30). What does it look like to grieve the Holy Spirit? One way Christians do this is by stretching the truth. That's the politically correct term for lying. And lying grieves the Holy Spirit. Second, borrowing without returning, otherwise known as stealing, grieves Him. He is grieved when we deface a person's character, otherwise known as gossip. We grieve Him with our unforgiveness, evidenced when we attempt to get even with those who have wronged us. The Holy Spirit says, "I grieve the loss of intimacy and closeness when you act in these ways. Stop it."

In 1 Thessalonians 5:19 Paul writes also, "Do not put out the spirit's fire." How do we do that? By studying the context of this verse, we see that we do this when we presume on God's grace, perhaps more easily understood as spiritual apathy—taking for granted the things of God. When we fail to walk our talk, we are guilty of hypocrisy, an act that puts out the Spirit's fire. The Holy Spirit cannot demonstrate His presence and power in a life that is cluttered with these things.

So let's review. How can you be filled with the Holy Spirit? Face the root of the problem. Invest your entire devotion. Look to Christ's cross. Live in humble obedience. The Holy Spirit will cleanse only the sin we confess. The Holy Spirit will fill only the life we consecrate. He will do His part. We must die to ourselves. When we offer our lives to Him, He will do His part. He'll cleanse our hearts. He will sanctify and fill us with His Holy Spirit.

FOUR

What About the Gifts of the Spirit?

IMAGINE it's Christmastime. When someone mentions the word "gift," what words come to your mind? *Free? Precious? Expression of love?* Everything we're likely to say about Christmas gifts is true about spiritual gifts as well. There's a lot of information out there about spiritual gifts. Some of it's true, and some of it's not. Some of it is stimulating; some of it's dangerous. So how can we distinguish between the good and the bad? My recommendation is that we stick with what God's Word tells us.

A good place to begin in seeking to understand about spiritual gifts is 1 Corinthians 12. In verse one Paul sets the table very intentionally: "Now about spiritual gifts, brothers, I do not want you to be ignorant." The original language for the term Paul uses here for "spiritual gifts" is *charismata*, the same word from which we derive the word "charisma." Sometimes when we hear the word "charisma," we think of a charismatic person, a person who's outgoing or has a dynamic personality. Other times we may think of the atmosphere of something, like the atmosphere of a restaurant or the atmosphere created when a certain style of music is played. To really get at the meaning of what Paul is talking about in 1 Corinthians 12:1, we must dismiss our presupposition of these meanings, because Paul is going a different direction.

The root word *charis* simply means "grace." And when used in its compound form as it is here, it means "grace gift." Spiritual gifts are grace gifts that God wants to bring to the heart of every believer for His purposes in the Church. A spiritual gift is a divine endowment, given purely as an expression of God's favor. It's given only at the discretion of God's sovereign grace. Spiritual gifts are not things we can earn. The best we can do is to receive them. And once we receive them, they should be developed.

It's helpful here for us to make a distinction between spiritual gifts and talents. The difference in these lies in the difference between common graces and special graces.[1] Common graces are natural abilities with which we are born—the natural disposition to excel at something—thinking logically or creatively, to sing or participate in sports at a high level. We've all been amazed at some individuals' abilities to take things apart and fix them or to perform some specific action that many of the rest of us are unable to do no matter how hard we try. We sometimes say they just have a knack for something. These gifts are called "common graces."

But spiritual gifts are different. These are present from the time of our spiritual birth, not our natural birth. This is the event Jesus was talking about when He said to Nicodemus, "No one can see the kingdom of God unless he is born again" (John 3:3). When we experience

---

1. I am indebted to my friend and colleague Dr. Jim Garlow at Skyline Wesleyan Church for this definition of common graces and special graces.

a spiritual birth, the Holy Spirit takes up residence in our lives and brings with Him a gifting of the Spirit. So talents are natural abilities, while spiritual gifts are spiritual endowments.

The man who heads up the security of our church building has a natural ability to provide great security, and everyone feels very comfortable knowing he is at work. As I've watched both his work and his life, I've seen that not only does he have natural ability but he's also a very effective pastor of his team. He loves those team members and is much more their pastor than I am. That's a supernatural endowment that God has entrusted to him. Do you see the difference between his natural talent and his spiritual gift?

Also, in seeing the difference between common graces and special graces, it is helpful to understand that their purposes are different. The purpose of a talent is for instruction, entertainment, or inspiration. We receive all of these when people share their talents with us. But spiritual gifts have a different purpose. They are for spiritual growth, individually and corporately. They're to build unity in the Body of Christ and for Christian service so the Church can fulfill God's purpose in the world. Instruction, entertainment, inspiration for *talents*, and spiritual growth and unity for *spiritual gifts*.

I've found this true in my own life. God has entrusted me with a natural musical talent. And I have a responsibility to develop that and use it for Him. I have a responsibility to keep that talent fresh and sharp so I can use it for God's glory. But I also have a responsibility to develop the spiritual gifts that the Holy Spirit brings into my life. One of my spiritual gifts is the gift of preaching. Those who know me realize this is not a natural ability for me. For a long time I avoided God's desire for this part of my life because I didn't see myself as a preacher. Yet it never ceases to amaze me when I stand before God's people that the miracle of preaching can happen—because He supernaturally empowers me to bring His message on a consistent basis.

Christians today largely get their understanding of spiritual gifts from three specific places in the New Testament: 1 Corinthians 12—14, Romans 12, and Ephesians 4. These passages list some specific examples of spiritual gifts, but many biblical scholars today believe that these lists are not exhaustive. They are simply representative of what the Holy Spirit wants to do. One of the reasons for this belief is that in the Early Church, as depicted in the Book of Acts, we see demonstrations of several gifts not mentioned in these other passages—gifts like intercession, compassion, and encouragement, just to name a few. These gifts that the Holy Spirit brings in through the Body of Christ as He's working through New Testament believers are not listed in any of these other passages. A second reason many believe these lists of gifts are not complete is that if they were meant as exhaustive lists, Paul would have mentioned the same gifts each time. But he doesn't; each time he gives just a representative listing.

A second important question we need to consider is "Who administers these gifts?" An interesting tidbit about the Bible is that there is no mention of spiritual gifts in the entire Old Testament. We find passages about the Holy Spirit, and see that He is at work—but nothing of what we find in the New Testament regarding spiritual gifts. The giving of spiritual gifts is a distinctively New Testament phenomenon. The first time we see them is in Acts 2 in the Upper Room when those one hundred twenty were gathered following Jesus' instructions to wait in Jerusalem for the gift of the Holy Spirit. Immediately we begin to see the evidence, the manifestation of spiritual gifts. Throughout the Book of Acts, when the apostles were first filled with the Holy Spirit, we discover that there's a connection between the coming of the Holy Spirit and the releasing of spiritual gifts. The Spirit is the one who administers the gifts.

It is critical to recognize that the Holy Spirit is the *only* one who gives spiritual gifts and that He gives only as He determines. In 1 Corinthians 12:11 we read, "All these are the work of one and the same Spirit, and he gives them to each one, just as he determines." This is the same Spirit whom Jesus was talking to His disciples about in John 14-16. It's the same Spirit that the apostle

Paul talks about in other New Testament writings, the Holy Spirit of God himself, whom the Father promised and who came at Pentecost and lives in the heart of every believer. He is the administrator of spiritual gifts. Even further, He gives as He determines.

We have nothing to do with the administration of spiritual gifts. It's not unusual to find certain believers who try to work themselves into some gift. They pray *Holy Spirit, give me this. I really want that. I see how you use that person over there. Could you give me that gift so I could do what he [she] does?* Yet the Spirit gives only as He determines, and He has it all figured out. If we seek a particular gift, we're likely to miss Him. But when we seek Him, He will bring everything into our lives that we need.

Another obvious question is "Who receives these gifts?" 1 Corinthians 12:7 tells us, "To each one the manifestation of the Spirit is given for the common good." Paul says it again in verse 11. So who is "each one"? Paul's letter is addressed to people who have placed their trust in Jesus Christ. So "each one" who is given spiritual gifts is *every* believer. To every believer around the world God has given some talents, which we have an obligation to use for His glory. But He's also given us spiritual gifts, and we have the same responsibility and privilege of developing those gifts and using them for the glory of God as well. You see, if we don't do what God has called us to do, the body hurts. Some need is not being met. Somebody else who is not equipped for it is going to try to do it. And he or she is not going to be as good as you are.

Recently, after moving to a new house, I was looking for something at home. You know how it is after you move—you have items in storage, in the basement, in the garage. When you don't move much, you have years to figure out where everything is. But I've moved recently, so not everything is currently easy to find. I was looking for something in my nightstand and found a sleeve of brand-new Titleist Pro-V1 golf balls. If you're a golfer, you know these are the best golf balls around and very expensive. Apparently someone gave me a sleeve of these some time back. I have no idea who, I have no idea when, but I was so afraid I was going to lose them that I stuck them in the nightstand—to be forgotten for an indefinite amount of time. The whole purpose of a golf ball is that it will help your game, not to sit in the nightstand. The application to spiritual gifts is clear—don't pretend you don't have a role to play in the Church. If you know Jesus Christ, you have a vital role to play. And God wants you to discover and develop the gifting in your life for His glory.

At the other extreme are people who want all the gifts. I appreciate their enthusiasm, but that's not what God has in mind for us. In 1 Corinthians 12:29-30 Paul asks a series of rhetorical questions. He says, "Are all apostles? Are all prophets? Are all teachers? Do all work miracles? Do all have gifts of healing? Do all speak in tongues? Do all interpret?" The answer is obviously no. And neither should it be expected.

It's one thing to desire spiritual gifts. It's quite another to presume that the Holy Spirit should give us all of them, or even that He should give us any particular gift. Remember: these are *gifts*, not awards. Every believer should expect to receive at least one gift. But no believer should expect to receive all the gifts. When we discover our individual gifts for the common good, we're forced to work together. We're dependent upon each other. And the Holy Spirit disperses these gifts, not only so the needs in that Body will be met but also so the Body of Christ will be working together.

Go back to the last part of verse 7 in 1 Corinthians 12. Notice that the manifestation of the Spirit is given for the common good. The test of any genuine manifestation of the Spirit of God is that it builds up, it strengthens, it fosters unity in the Church. If the result of something we think of as a gift is confusion or divisiveness, then we must soundly reject it as not being a gift of the Spirit. The Holy Spirit brings unity. He brings strengthening in the body.

This was a problem in the Corinthian church to whom Paul was writing. The people were what some have termed "carnal Christians." Carnal Christians are people who have invited the Holy Spirit into their lives but still insist on being in control. I was talking to a man recently who said he lived most of his life this way. He said he was ninety-five-percent committed but that there was one little place he still wanted to have some control. And he told me that until he died out to that, he was a carnal Christian. God couldn't use him then the way He's using him now. God is using him powerfully today. Carnal Christians have been born of the spirit, but they are not yet filled with the Spirit. Their sins have been forgiven, but their sinful egos have not been conquered. They are self-centered, not Christ-centered.

It's a dangerous thing for carnal Christians to try to work out the gifts of Spirit in their lives, because their focus and emphasis are still on themselves. It's all about them, their ego, their needs. But this approach won't work with spiritual gifts.

Look at Paul's exhortation 1 Corinthians 14:12: "Since you are eager to have spiritual gifts, try to excel in gifts that build up the church." Again, in verse 26 he underscores it by saying, "All of these must be done for the strengthening of the church." Any manifestation that does not build unity in the church is not of the Holy Spirit.

Before we leave this discussion on spiritual gifts, we must look at what makes it all operate smoothly. If you have an engine that doesn't have any oil in it, what happens? It's going to lock up—friction heats up until the whole thing just stops working. That happens in relationships, too. And look at how Paul handles that. See what

Paul puts between the twelfth and fourteenth chapters of 1 Corinthians—the famous love chapter, 1 Corinthians 13. Love is the oil that makes spiritual gifts work together. In fact Paul wraps up chapter 12 by writing, "And now I will you show you the most excellent way." All this other stuff we've been talking about hinges on this. Love is the key. You can offer up all kinds of acts of service, you can have all knowledge, you can boast of numerous gifts and abilities, but if there isn't love, it doesn't amount to anything. Why is love the key? Because love is the fruit of the Spirit. Love is the highest of all standards. If we do everything in love, the Holy Spirit can work it all out for God's glory and for the benefit of everyone involved. Love is the fruit of the Spirit that brings credibility to the gifts of the Spirit. When love is your motive, the Holy Spirit can work unhindered through you.

How Can I Bear the
Fruit of the Holy Spirit?

THE LITMUS TEST of a life led and controlled by the Spirit of God is not in the words we say but rather in the fruit of our lives. This is what Jesus meant when He said, "By their fruit you will recognize them. Do people pick grapes from thorn bushes, or figs from thistles? Likewise every good tree bears good fruit, but a bad tree bears bad fruit" (Matthew 7:16-17). Jesus is saying that if we really want to know whether we're living a life controlled by His Spirit, check the fruit.

What is the fruit of the Spirit? In the fifth chapter of Galatians Paul contrasts a life of bad fruit with a life filled with good fruit. And he simply lists the good fruit: "The fruit of the Spirit is love, joy, peace, patience, kindness, goodness, faithfulness, gentleness, and self-control. Against such things there is no law" (Galatians 5:22-23). Now the apostle Paul is talking about an entire cluster, a cornucopia so to speak. He doesn't focus on any one particular fruit. He could talk about love. He could talk about joy and patience and kindness. He could unpack those things for us here, but that's not what He does. His point is not to say, "Christian, make this your goal. Strive for this every day." No, He simply states that this is the natural product of a Christian life. This is the natural result of a life that is led and controlled by the Holy Spirit. Spiritual fruit is not a work. It's not something that we do for God. That's why I've titled this chapter "How Can I *Bear* the Fruit of the Holy Spirit?" rather than "How

72

Can I *Produce* the Fruit of the Holy Spirit?" The fruit of the Holy Spirit is what He produces in and through me, not what I produce for Him. I can't produce anything for God. As a branch connected to the vine (Jesus Christ), my part is simply to bear what He is producing in me.

What happens if you say, "I'm going to be more loving in my life this week"? It's not long before you've said something you shouldn't have said, right? If you say, "I'm going to have peace," what do you do? You start worrying. Whenever we try to do these things, we fail every time. That's what Paul is trying to say here. The key idea is that spiritual fruit is not the product of our own efforts. We lower God's fruit standard to a work standard when what we *do* becomes more important than who we *are*. The Holy Spirit is much more interested in our character than He is in our accomplishments. That's not to say that we don't do anything. It just means that unless what we do for Christ flows out of who we are in Christ, there will never be spiritual fruit.

Paul reinforces this in Galatians chapter five when he tells us the Spirit-filled life is not defined by what we do for God, because "those who belong to Christ Jesus have crucified the sinful nature" (Galatians 5:24). To be Spirit-filled there has to be a death to self. We must face the root of the problem. We don't need one more Band-Aid in our lives. We don't need one more book on positive thinking. We don't need one more how-to manual. We

73

need a radical dying-out of ourselves deep in our spirits so that we can walk according to His Spirit.

So Paul says that when this happens, when we crucify that self-centered ego, then the Holy Spirit can begin to flow freely in our lives, and the result of that is spiritual fruit. Again, it's not what we *do* for Him—rather, it's what we allow God to do in and through us.

In the next verse Paul goes on to affirm, "Since we live by the Spirit, let us keep in step with the Spirit." I love the word picture Paul uses: *keep in step with the Spirit.* You see, the Holy Spirit produces spiritual fruit in my life as I cooperate with Him. I don't get ahead of Him; neither do I passively lag behind him. I must keep in step with the rhythms of God's Spirit in my life. As I do that, I begin to see fruit coming out of my life—spiritual fruit, good fruit. Learn to practice the presence of the Holy Spirit in your life. Trust Him. Begin to move out and trust those promptings He's placing in your life. Stay in step with the Spirit. Stay in the Word.

It's very difficult for us to do this, because we live in such a work-oriented culture. We're very pragmatic. We live in a society where people's worth and value are determined by what they do more than who they are. When you meet people for the first time, probably in the first minute or two you've asked what they do for a living. It's one of the first things we want to find out. We define people more by what they do than by who they are. We lower the "fruit standard" to this "work standard" when we define the Spirit-filled life by what we do. For example, most people would agree that it's easier to help out by serving in ministry in your church than it is to love your enemies. See, you can serve in church and still harbor bitterness toward somebody. It's easier to do something physical than it is to forgive. It's easier to fill our lives with activities for God than it is to come to grips with our devotion to God.

I must confess that it's easier to write a chapter on the fruit of the Spirit than it is to be patient when things don't go the way I think they should. Do you see the difference between the work standard and the fruit standard? It's easier to serve God than it is to be kind to someone who has just verbally assaulted you. That's the difference. As stated before, we want to define our Spirit-filled lives by what we do, but spiritual fruit does not come from work.

Spiritual fruit is also not a gift. We lower God's fruit standard to a gift standard when our experience becomes more important than our character. Personal experience is the highest authority in our culture right now. In answer to the question "What is truth?" most people today would say it's whatever we want it to be. Yet this is a very dangerous understanding of our world, because experiences are just like our emotions—they're fickle things. If our truth is based upon whatever our circumstances are at any given moment, it leaves us without any objective anchor in our lives. We're just kind of floating around. So experience has trumped the truth of character.

Character is something outside us. It's what God builds in us, but it is based upon what happens outside us. The character of our lives is based upon the historical reality of Christ's death and resurrection on the Cross. That's the anchor, not our fickle experience, not what we feel at any given moment. It's on the reality that Jesus Christ died and rose again on the third day and is alive. That is the basis of truth. Now our character comes as we build our lives on that foundation. The Spirit-filled life is not defined by what gift we have received or by what experience we have had. Rather, it is defined by what gifts we share with others out of the character of Christ in our lives.

Would you not agree that it's easier to seek some spiritual gift than it is to forgive someone who has deeply hurt you? Would you not agree that it's easier to get people to come to a miracle healing rally than it is to get them to be faithful to the Lord in ministry week in, week out, year in, year out? See, we like the gifts. We like the sensations. But God is interested in building character. He's interested in the fruit of our lives. The fruit standard is a higher standard than the gift standard.

When there's no difference in the way God's people live and the way the world lives, then Christians have no credibility to a lost world. Yet there are many who realize that there is a connection to God in the way we treat our spouses, raise our kids, spend our money, invest our time. These things make all the difference in living a Spirit-led life. But the world wants nothing to do with a Christian who says one thing on Sunday and lives just like the world throughout the week. Spiritual fruit is Christlike character. Character has more to do with the motive of our hearts than it does the work we do or the gifts we possess. When the fruit of the Spirit is evident in our conduct and lifestyles, then the world will receive our work, and the Church will trust our gifts. Spiritual fruit is the litmus test.

So if that's the case, how does God produce the fruit of the Spirit in our lives? Just see what Jesus says in John 15:5: "I am the vine; you are the branches. If a man remains in me and I in him, he will bear much fruit; apart from me you can nothing." Apart from the vine, from Jesus, His Spirit, you can't do anything. It's not going to be of any value. See—it's not about experience. It's not about a gift. It's not about a work standard. It's about a *relationship*. You must be in right relationship with the Spirit. Remember: it's not your efforts to create love, your efforts to create joy or peace or patience that produce spiritual fruit. A branch cannot do anything unless it's tied in to the trunk, the life nutrients.

Notice how God responds to those who bear good fruit. He says in John 15 that every branch that bears fruit is pruned so that it will bear even more fruit. So the right result is bearing more and better, sweeter, juicier, spiritual fruit. But notice what Jesus says about how the Father treats the branches that are not fruitful: "He is thrown away as a branch and dries up; and they gather them, and cast them into the fire and they are burned" (John 15:6, NASB).

In my garden I find these little branches I call *suckers.* They're these little branches of the tree, but they grow near the bottom of the trunk, and there's never any fruit on them. I know if I want to get more fruit out of that plant, I have to cut off the suckers. Jesus talks about those of us who play that role in our spiritual lives when He says He will cut off the branches that do not bear fruit. If you claim to be a Christian but there's no spiritual fruit evident in your life, it won't be long before you'll find yourself completely cut off from the vine. Every branch gets cut on. It's our choice as to whether that cutting is going to be pruning, which will make us more productive, or is going to cut us off completely. So we need to stay connected to the vine. And if we do, this leads to the last point—that the right result is enduring spiritual fruit.

Jesus says in John 15:16, "I chose you and appointed you to go and bear fruit—fruit that will last." Think about that. God chose you. Jesus looked down the corridors of time and said, "I choose you. I can produce this fruit in a myriad of ways, but I want to choose you to bear My fruit." What a privilege to be one of God's branches! He believes in you. He appointed you. And remember that it's not about you. You just make yourself available for Him to flow through.

Think about that last phrase, too: "fruit that will last." Scripture tells us that everything we do is going to be burned up. And one day, when Jesus comes back, we won't need spiritual gifts anymore, because we'll see Him as He is. We'll know Him even as we are fully known. But the fruit of the Spirit goes on forever.

So the first question we must ask ourselves is "What do our branches look like?" Is there anything in our lives blocking the ability of the Holy Spirit to flow through us? We get so good at rationalizing away the things that hinder the Holy Spirit. We must work to stay sensitive to Him so we can answer this question. Is there any area of disobedience where we have ignored or resisted His voice? If so, we must confess that to Him, acknowledge what He already knows. We must repent of that sin and once again release our control.

The second question we must ask ourselves is this: "Is the fruit of our lives evidence of the flow of God's Spirit through us? Is there fruit?" Refer again to Galatians 5:22-23: "The fruit of the Spirit is love, joy, peace, patience, kindness, goodness, faithfulness, gentleness and self-control." Are our lives characterized by these things? If I asked your spouse, what would your spouse say? If I asked your kids, "Is Dad kind? Is Dad good? Is Dad patient? Is Dad joyful? Is Mom loving? Is there self-control there?" What would they say? What would your friends say? And when you realize there are areas keeping this fruit from growing in your life, then the Spirit will have made available to you the next stage for your spiritual growth and development.

What Is the Impact of a Spirit-filled Life?

I RECENTLY heard about a woman who had a bad day to beat all bad days. She was on her way to work, frantic because she was late. Her anxieties were building when she pulled up in a left turn lane behind another driver and waited, waited, and waited. Finally the light turned green, but the man's car just sat there. In her frustration, the woman began honking. But the man's car still just sat. She became so agitated that she rolled down the window and started yelling at the man.

She finally got his attention, and he drove on through the turn just as it was turning red, forcing her to miss the turn for one more light. As she was sitting there contemplating having to wait for another light, she finally exploded. She started swearing and yelling at the other driver, waving her arms and beating on the steering wheel. Anyone in another car might have thought she was mentally disturbed. As she finally made the turn after the next green light, she looked in her rear-view mirror to see flashing police lights behind her. Before she even really knew what was happening, she had been arrested and taken to the police station.

After an hour or so, the arresting officer came to her, apologizing profusely: "Ma'am, I am so sorry. I need to apologize to you. We've had a case of mistaken identity; I thought you were someone else. When I pulled up behind your car and saw the way you were acting, then noticed you had one of those little Christian fish and a

'What would Jesus do?' sticker on your bumper, I just assumed the car was stolen!"

How many times in our lives has this been us? Maybe it's not always such an obvious action, but sometimes we think we're showing discretion when everyone around us recognizes we're doing anything but.

Few Christians would argue with the idea that God wants our lives to have a positive impact for Him. In fact Jesus said, "I tell you the truth, anyone who has faith in me will do what I have been doing. He will do even greater things than these, because I am going to the Father" (John 14:12). What are the kinds of things Jesus did while He walked on this earth? He healed the sick, He gave sight to the blind, He raised the dead. He served others, He was generous, He gave of himself, He fed the five thousand. Jesus says anyone who believes in Him can do greater works than these. Now that's what I call an impact! But how can this be? Well, the key is in that last phrase: ". . . because I am going to the Father." Remember how Jesus told the disciples that until He left the earth the Holy Spirit could not come? Well, the same Spirit who lived inside Jesus when He walked this earth two thousand years ago is living in every child of God today.

In Luke 24:49 Jesus begins to describe this power of God: "I am going to send you what my father has promised; but stay in the city until you have been clothed with power from on high." The first thing to notice about this passage is that this power of God originates outside us.

There are two prevailing philosophies in our culture today regarding power. The most popular one tells us that our power originates from within us. It tells us that if we just look down deep inside, we'll find this untapped power, and we have to learn how to lock into that. We hear a lot of this kind of talk coming from self-realization gurus and self-help books. Secular humanism and the New Age Movement tell us it's all about us and that we just need to tap into secret parts of our power and cultivate it.

The less popular philosophy of power is that it comes from outside of us, and this is the idea that the Bible supports. The Bible tells us our power is not from within but from on high. It tells us that it's only as we look to Christ and trust in His Spirit to rule in our lives that we can experience His supernatural power. As believers, as children of God, we have the choice to tap into this power every day. But if we don't know Jesus Christ, we don't have that choice.

What this means for us is that when we're tempted we have this power outside us that we can rely on to get us through. Just because we're filled with the Holy Spirit doesn't mean we aren't tempted. As a matter of fact, when we're children of God the temptations often come at us harder than if we didn't call God our Father. But when we're tempted, we can either face the temptation in our own strength and try to fight the devil with our own abilities, or we can rely on the power from the Holy Spirit living in us.

Many times when we're going through trials we just grit our teeth and try to muscle through. We take a grin-and-bear-it mentality. And every time we do that, we're crushed under the weight of the trial. But when we call on the name of the Lord and ask Him to use His power in us, He gives us the grace and strength to get through those trials. We don't need to be in control but to be under the Spirit's control.

Jesus' own disciples are a great example of these differences in power. Throughout His ministry when Jesus talked about this power, the disciples didn't get it. When He was preaching the kingdom of God, the disciples thought it was going to be an earthly kingdom, so they reacted in the way the world does. James and John—when the Samaritans were criticizing Jesus—suggested that Jesus call down fire on them. That was their way to deal with a bad situation. That was their idea of power. When Jesus was arrested, what did Peter do? He pulled out a sword, and he went after Malcus, cutting off his ear. That's the earthly way to exert power. But after all this happened, forty days after Jesus had ascended to heaven, the disciples were in the Upper Room in Jerusalem—and the Holy Spirit came in power. It was a new kind of power. This power from on high, a spiritual power, filled their lives.

Finally we see some radical changes in these guys. Now we see Peter is in a courtyard in Jerusalem talking to the same guys who had just nailed Jesus to the Cross: "You killed the Son of God. You need to repent." Where had the man gone who had disowned Jesus during his inquisition because he was afraid for his life? This new power created a radical change in him. This is the change the Holy Spirit, a spiritual power, makes in our lives today. When the disciples received the power of the Spirit, they overcame hate with love. They overcame the world because of the Cross. A symbol of defeat became a symbol of victory. They believed that mercy is stronger than might, that love is stronger than the law, that offering forgiveness is stronger than holding a grudge, that faith is stronger than fear. They had been changed from the inside out! A spiritual power, this power of God, had taken over their lives.

In the first chapter of Acts Jesus tells those gathered with Him not to leave Jerusalem. Then a few verses later He said, "You will receive power when the Holy Spirit comes on you; and you will be my witnesses in Jerusalem, and in all Judea and Samaria, and to the ends of the earth." This is an interesting juxtaposition of two thoughts. First, it's natural when we're feeling burdened and need to be renewed to want to get away. We want to go somewhere and get our heads clear. But Jesus specifically told the disciples not to do that. He said to wait right there in the city. The city is where all the problems were, the center of all the stresses and headaches, tensions, and temptations, pressing responsibilities and relationships. This is an interesting way for Jesus to give the message that God's power is sufficient for life's toughest challenges.

There's something else interesting here. Christ wasn't generic about saying to stay where people are. He said to stay in Jerusalem. At this point in the disciples' lives Jerusalem represented crucifixion, the death of a dream. This is where they saw Jesus suffer what appeared to be their greatest defeat. But Jesus said, "No. You guys wait right here in Jerusalem for the indwelling Holy Spirit. I'm going to turn this place—the place that's been your greatest defeat—into a place of my greatest triumph." "Stay right here," Jesus said. "I'm going to show you incredible power."

This is where we need to live. This is the power to live victoriously. When a watching world sees in the midst of our stresses and problems that we have peace, we have joy, we have victory, they're going to say, "Hey—I want that too. What's the source of that?" There's our opportunity. This power is strength, not just to live victoriously but also to witness effectively. The disciples were scared to death. Jesus was gone. They were behind closed doors there in Jerusalem. And the only thing that could get them out from behind those closed doors and into the streets was the power of God's Holy Spirit.

When I look across the worldwide Church today, I see a lot of programs. I see a lot of activity. I see a lot of talk and a lot of noise. But I don't see a lot of God's power working through people to bring the lost to Him. Like the disciples living behind doors of fear, today many of us limit God's Spirit in our lives because we're locked behind doors of fear too.

The world is a scary place—nobody is going to argue about that. Just turn on the news, and you see all kinds of scary stuff. So in fear we justify our safe, secure religious bubbles surrounded by our nice, loving Christian friends. But it's fear that's driving us. We need the Holy Spirit to thrust us out from behind these doors of fear into a lost and hurting world. That's where the joy is.

We also are often imprisoned behind doors of compromise. A watching world sees what we say, they hear what we sing, they watch our religious programs on Sunday, then they watch us during the week—and see that our lifestyle is no different than theirs. There's no evidence that our marriages are any different or that we regard our money any differently.

But if we die to ourselves, our lives become all about Him. That's what made the New Testament Christians so powerful. They literally changed their world in one generation. They discovered that God's power, its purpose, is to embolden the most fearful disciple. Today millions of Christians are scared to death to be bold for Christ. Living the Spirit-filled life is about God igniting a passion in our hearts that will not fade so that a watching world can say, "That's God there. That's not the flesh—it's passion." And when that passion takes over, look what can happen: on the day of Pentecost one hundred twenty people walked out of that room with the power of the Holy Spirit, and about three thousand people came to a saving knowledge of Jesus Christ that day.

Jesus said, "Greater works than I have done you will do." We never saw three thousand people at once come to God through Jesus during His time on earth. This is an example of God doing greater things through those who believe in Him. This Spirit-filled life is about a big God working through you to bring people to Him. This is the purpose of God's power.

Unfortunately, not everybody gets it. Some people try to pervert God's power because they still think it's about them. We see an example of this in Acts 8. Simon was a man who loved the occult and working magic; what he really loved was himself, but he used the occult and magic to stoke his ego. He heard the message of the gospel, and he turned to Christ. He opened his heart and accepted Jesus Christ, but he still had an infatuation with all the signs and the wonders he had been able to perform through demonic powers. He was focused on that.

Look at what happens in Acts 8:18-19: "When Simon saw that the Spirit was given at the laying on of the apostles' hands, he offered them money and said, 'Give me also this ability so that everyone on whom I lay my hands may receive the Holy Spirit.'" And how did Peter respond? "May your money perish with you, because you thought you could buy the gift of God with money! You have no part or share in this ministry, because your heart is not right before God" (verses 20-21). His heart wasn't right. Because he had the wrong focus, his heart was still corrupt.

Are we like that? Have we accepted the claims of Christ but still live with corrupt hearts? Earlier we talked about carnal Christians. This is an example of what carnal Christians do regarding spiritual gifts—they try to manipulate them to their own benefit. But the purpose of spiritual gifts is to build unity in the Church. Here we see Simon trying to distort the power of God in the same way. He wanted to use it for his own benefit.

We see at least two distortions of truth in Simon's story. The first is a distortion of truth based on religious ritual. Simon observed that the Holy Spirit was given by the laying on of hands, so he said, "Hey, if I just do the same thing, maybe I can produce the same result." This is what distorted religion does—it tries to manage God's power. People with a distorted religion see God work in a supernatural way on a specific occasion and think that's how God has to work all the time.

But God is bigger than our religious traditions. God is not limited by any kind of methodology. He is a creative God who has a thousand different ways to accomplish His will and purpose. Distorted religion focuses on external things because it's easier than emphasizing the heart. Only God can see what's happening in our hearts, and some people don't like that. So they emphasize the outward things instead.

Second, Simon's motivation was not only from religious ritual but also from personal gain. He tried to manipulate God's power because of his pride. If religious tradition tries to manage God's power, pride tries to manipulate it for its own ends. God's power flows from His heart to a believer's humble and broken heart. To anyone who tries to pervert it or misuse it, Peter says, "You have no part in this ministry."

We think of power in our human mind-set, with our cultural perspective. We believe that if we're going to be powerful, we have to look powerful and have all the trappings. But this is just the opposite of God's power. In 2 Corinthians 4:7 Paul tells us about it when he writes, "We have this treasure in jars of clay to show that this all-surpassing power is from God and not from us." Those jars of clay are us. They're clay because they're nothing special, not deserving of any particular honor. The place of power is in our weakness. God is telling us that He does His best work when we're at our weakest, when we're the least qualified. In my own life I see this in my preaching. It's in preaching that I feel least qualified to do God's work. Yet I see that this is where God does His most effective work through my life.

It's meaningful that we hear these words in Scripture coming from Paul. He wasn't just preaching them—he was living them. In 2 Corinthians 12 we find him giving his personal testimony about this very thing. Paul was an incredible man. He had an impressive pedigree and a lot of earthly power he could leverage. Yet he says that to keep him from becoming conceited he had a thorn in his flesh; some recurring problem that would not go away. Scholars have speculated for centuries about what this problem was; some think it was a physical impediment—blindness perhaps. Other have surmised other things. In the end we really don't know what his thorn was. Paul says God allowed this thorn in his flesh to remain. He called the thorn a "messenger of Satan." God didn't cause it, but He allowed it to remain.

Paul prayed repeatedly for God to take it away. "Three times I pleaded with the Lord to take it away from me." Essentially God said, "Paul, you're not seeing this right. My grace is sufficient for you to go on living successfully despite this problem." How do we know God's grace is sufficient for us to live successfully while problems exist in our lives? Because His power is made perfect in weakness. Weakness is where His power resides in us. In verse nine Paul says that in light of all this, if it's all about God, it's not about Paul. If it's about God bringing glory, and He can bring greater glory through the thorns in the flesh, then we should boast all the more gladly about our weaknesses so that Christ's power may rest on us. This is a great mystery to those outside the kingdom of God; the Bible sounds like gibberish to non-Christians who hear verses like 2 Corinthians 12:10—"For when I am weak, then I am strong."

For those who are God's children, we realize that there are going to be times when we are absolutely overwhelmed and inadequate. It's in times like this that we remember how God's power works—when we are weak, then we're strong, because His power is made perfect in those times. The times when we feel the weakest are when God does His most powerful work.

This is not just theology; this is not just preaching or teaching. God wants to make an important impact through your life. What is the impact of your life? If you were convicted for being a disciple of Christ, would there be enough evidence against you to support that claim?

It is my prayer that you will experience the presence and power of the Holy Spirit every day. Don't try to live the Christian life without Him. As you release the controls of your life to Him, you will discover the joy and fulfillment of a life led by the Holy Spirit. And as you do, a watching world will witness the impact of a Spirit-filled life and be drawn to Him.